T0196070

IMPRESSIONS

For Such a Time as This (Esther 4:14, KJV)

Gale Alvarez

WESTBOW
PRESS®
A DIVISION OF THOMAS NELSON
& ZONDERVAN

WestBow Press books may be ordered through
booksellers or by contacting:

WestBow Press
A Division of Thomas Nelson & Zondervan
1663 Liberty Drive
Bloomington, IN 47403
www.westbowpress.com
1 (866) 928-1240

Because of the dynamic nature of the Internet, any web
addresses or links contained in this book may have changed
since publication and may no longer be valid. The views
expressed in this work are solely those of the author and do
not necessarily reflect the views of the publisher, and the
publisher hereby disclaims any responsibility for them.

Any people depicted in stock imagery provided by Thinkstock
are models,
and such images are being used for illustrative purposes only.
Certain stock imagery © Thinkstock.

ISBN: 978-1-9736-0554-6 (sc)
ISBN: 978-1-9736-0553-9 (e)

Library of Congress Control Number: 2017916101

Print information available on the last page.

WestBow Press rev. date: 03/08/2018

This book of impressions is dedicated to my son, Josh, and to my brother, Steven.

Joshua Kenneth came into my life when he was three days old. I took him home the day I met him, and I knew that keeping him was going to be one of the greatest fights of my life. I had to rush Josh to the hospital the day after he was placed in my arms as I was told he was going to die.

It took months of constant care, many doctors' appointments, and lots of isolation, as I stood fighting for him to live. I am eternally grateful that in the end God gets the last word, and after many weeks in the hospital, Josh was released.

I dedicated Josh to the Lord when he was four months old. In the midst of a long, drawn-out fight, I was told we were not going to win, but God sovereignly turned it all around, and I finally was able to adopt him. To this day, I still weep when I think of the honor I have been given to be his mom. I love you, Josh, and am so very proud of the man of God you are and the legacy you are embracing. You are a son of honor, and greater works than I have ever done, you will do to the glory of God.

Steven Robert came into my life when I was twenty-one years old. There were twins in his mother's womb, and Steven was the only one to survive.

I have watched him fight some of life's greatest battles, and with the help of God and prayer, I see him standing on top of every mountain that was sent to crush him. Steven is and has a strong voice; when he sings, I hear in him the voice of our dad, who died of AIDs and never had the opportunity to value or appreciate the son born from his loins.

I love Steven as though he were my son. In fact, I call him my brother/son. What pain and joy we have shared in life's journey together. In the bitter and in the sweet times, we have learned to cling to the cross and to stay anchored in the one who gave His life for us. I love you, Steven, and I will never cease to pray for you or to give thanks for you. Your best days are in front of you, and that is something I know for sure. You will fulfill all of God's will for your life, leaving a destined legacy with nothing undone.

Endorsement

Jesus said that His purpose for coming to earth was to give us life and life more abundantly (John 10:10). Why is it then that so many believers find the enemy robbing their vision, stealing their gifts, and destroying their hopes?

Impressions offers hope as Gale Alvarez takes you by the hand and heart into Spirit-filled reflections woven together with God's sure word that will lead you into the abundant life the Lord makes available through His ever- present, inexhaustible grace and mercy.

Gale will be the first to tell you that she has been drawn and captivated by His unfailing love, and now she shares this all-powerful, overflowing God with her readers who have ears to hear and hearts to receive a blessed and endless hope.

Wisdom and humility are brought together in these timeless impressions written by a servant whose desire is to love Jesus in deep ways, with a longing to reflect a grateful life that will lead others to experience God's merciful love.

Gale's insightful *Impressions* express life-changing power that will bring you to a place of humility where you shake off thoughts of lack, impossibility, and despair for a better promise as you begin to realize a renewed life of possibility designed by God, especially for you.

Dr. Dawn Chillon, PhD, LPC
founder, The Foundation for Family Healing

Contents

Foreword

As a writer, I am very excited about the inspirational collection of impressions contained inside this book. I have known author and Pastor Gale Alvarez for many years and understand what it takes to go inside of yourself and be transparent enough to pour out something of sustenance to enhance the lives of others. It is no easy task. Many start out on this road with good intentions, but few cross the finish line.

What qualifies a writer? As the saying goes, "You can't tell anyone about a place you've never been." That's why testimonies and testimonials are so powerful. They allow one to juxtapose a life experience to a safe place where others can be influenced by it.

To be able to be touched by the journey of another because of his or her desire to help you is immeasurable. It comes from a place of unconditional love. *It's the overcoming of insurmountable odds that draws one to share the fruits of one's experience and another to take it in—a place where you don't have to go to or go through to learn the lesson, because someone else has already been there and done that before you.*

Being given the opportunity to learn from someone else's struggle is a blessing—much like Christ's struggle to set the captives free. All that's required is an open heart and an open mind to receive it.

A native of New Jersey, Pastor Gale Alvarez has been through some things. The place where she is now is not the same place she came from. She's had an amazing and inspirational journey. As a wife, mother, and copastor, she is a survivor and an overcomer. She has been tried by fire yet stands today shining bright like a diamond.

In 1977 Pastor Gale Alvarez invited Christ into her life, and like most of us, she jumped in with both feet and swam through turbulent waters, past an enemy whose assignment was to not let go. But God had the final say.

Pastor Gale is a woman of strong faith with an attitude of gratitude. Being grateful for God's love and what He has done in her life has enabled her to tap into the pulse of others' needs and concerns. Many lives have already been greatly impacted; because of her experiences and relationship with God, she is able to spiritually discern and address in her writings the many simple and complex issues people face daily.

When you can see yourself in the pages of a book, it becomes a mirror, reflective of your past and present and a portal into your future.

Writing is a gift God gave Pastor Gale as a tool to share her impressions of a life worth living.

The pages of this book contain building blocks of prose cemented with scripture. Inspirational and encouraging words are compassionately used to build up and fortify those who are searching, feeling lost, hurting, or just want *more* of Him. This book is made up of impressions birthed out of God's love for you.

Where are you today? Where do you want to be? What are the desires of your heart? What are you meditating on day and night?

On each page of *Impressions* lies a nugget or a jewel to be read and taken in—a rhema word, *"for such a time as this."*

Is the rhythm of your heartbeat aligned with the heartbeat of God, the Creator of life, the one who holds the key? I invite you to read, study, meditate, and absorb daily the impressions on each page, and then share these impressions through your voice with someone else.

As these words and scriptures become manna for your days, pay them forward, and I guarantee you, your life and someone else's life will never ever be the same.

Valerie J. Fullilove
writer/producer, Trinity Park Productions

Dear reader,

How beautiful the journey of a book, and what a wonder that you are now holding it in your hands.

I believe that we are at a place in life that scripture calls, "*for such a time as this.*" We have all been through and are going through stuff, yet in the midst of it all, there are life lessons to be learned and much we can learn from each other.

The book, *Impressions,* is a collection of thoughts birthed from my book *HeartBeats*, written with the hope to help you navigate your course. I have found life to be a winding road, and as I allow all roads to lead me to Him, I am impressed to continue with Him as the journey moves on.

We all need an anchor in life, and He is that faithful, loving anchor that holds, teaching me that through it all I can trust Him.

As a teacher, I always prepare my lesson understanding that my heartfelt desire is to leave my students with a word that goes deep, leaving them with an impression that speaks to each one individually. As a writer, I pray the same for each reader. You are here "*for such a time as this.*" *Gale Alvarez*

Above All Else

I want my life to speak
of relationship with Him
and then with humanity,
serving as many as
I can while I can.

*Jesus replied: "Love the Lord your God
with all your heart and with all your soul
and with all your mind. This is the first and
greatest commandment. And the second
is like it: Love your neighbor as yourself."*

(Matthew 22:37–39, NIV)

Surrender It

When you give Him the impossible, He will bring you the possible.

I am the LORD, the God of all mankind. Is anything too hard for me?

(Jeremiah 32:27, NIV)

Treasures

When we think about what we value, it's easy to see where our hearts are.

But store up for yourselves treasures in heaven, where neither moth nor rust destroys, and where thieves do not break in or steal; for where your treasure is, there your heart will be also.

(Matthew 6:20–21, NASB)

Faith Lights the World

Faith is a sign and a wonder to a world that needs to know.

Arise, shine, for your light has come, and the glory of the LORD has risen upon you.

(Isaiah 60:1, ESV)

Which Way?

Each time I face a
decision, I see a gate
that will take me on a
path. It is then that I must
choose the wide or the
narrow, for they both lead
me to a different place.

*Who, then, are those who fear the
LORD? He will instruct them in the
ways they should choose.*

(Psalm 25:12, NIV)

Move On

I see too many holding
on to yesterday and
bringing it into their
tomorrows, not realizing
that it is keeping
them from living in
their fullness today.

*Forget the former things; do not dwell on
the past. See, I am doing a new thing!
Now it springs up; do you not perceive
it? I am making a way in the wilderness
and streams in the wasteland.*

(Isaiah 43:18–19, NIV)

No Regrets

If we are going to live
a no-regret life, we
must make peace
with our past by giving
Him all the pieces.

*My old self has been crucified with
Christ. It is no longer I who live, but
Christ lives in me. So I live in this earthly
body by trusting in the Son of God, who
loved me and gave himself for me.*

(Galatians 2:20, NLT)

Wanna Make a Difference?

If we are going to make a difference in the earth, then we must know that the difference in us is Him.

To them God has chosen to make known among the Gentiles the glorious riches of this mystery, which is Christ in you, the hope of glory.

(Colossians 1:27, NIV)

From Here to Eternity

Our lives are a brief period of existence, and we cannot allow ourselves to become indifferent to the things that count for eternity.

Search me, God, and know my heart;
test me and know my anxious thoughts.
See if there is any offensive way in me,
and lead me in the way everlasting.

(Psalm 139:23–24, NIV)

Find Peace

I am learning to travel inward, into that perfect place of peace where I find Him and Him alone.

Neither shall they say, Lo here! or, lo there! for, behold, the kingdom of God is within you.

(Luke 17:21, KJV)

Within

It's hard to think when
your head is clogged
and hard to hear when
your ears hurt from all the
pressure and clanging.

*He that dwelleth in the secret place
of the most High shall abide under
the shadow of the Almighty.*

(Psalm 91:1, KJV)

Find Someone to Love

In every day there's a mouth to feed, a heart to touch, a need to supply, a person to love.

Feed the hungry, and help those in trouble. Then your light will shine out from the darkness, and the darkness around you will be as bright as noon.

(Isaiah 58:10, NLT)

Radiate Christ

I will forever sing of
His love, tell of His
goodness, and seek
to be an expression
of Him in this earth.

*The Spirit of the Lord is on me, because
he has anointed me to proclaim good news
to the poor. He has sent me to proclaim
freedom for the prisoners and recovery of
sight for the blind, to set the oppressed free,
to proclaim the year of the Lord's favor.*

(Luke 4:18–19, NIV)

Be There

When you leave someone's presence, make sure he or she knows you were there.

In the same way, let your light shine before others, that they may see your good deeds and glorify your Father in heaven.

(Matthew 5:16, NIV)

I Hear Him

His sound is so gentle, so firm, so real, so kind, so present; all in a whisper I hear His essence.

My sheep hear my voice, and I know them, and they follow me.

(John 10:27, ESV)

He Keeps Counting

Some days you can
think you are down
for the count, and
then you realize that
He keeps counting.

*Being confident of this, that he who began
a good work in you will carry it on to
completion until the day of Christ Jesus.*

(Philippians 1:6, NIV)

No Blurred Lines

God meant what He said and He said what He meant, and His Word is forever settled.

Thy word is a lamp unto my feet, and a light unto my path.

(Psalm 119:105, KJV)

Think Twice

As I react with others,
I often catch myself
thinking, Is this how I want
to be treated? Is this how
I want God to treat me?

Do not let kindness and truth leave you;
Bind them around your neck, Write
them on the tablet of your heart.

(Proverbs 3:3, NASB)

Make Room

Learning the lesson of
unpacking my mind
with stuff I should not
take with me when He
creates a space for me
to embrace renewal
is one of the greatest
lessons I've ever learned.

*This means that anyone who belongs to
Christ has become a new person. The
old life is gone; a new life has begun!*

(2 Corinthians 5:17, NLT)

Are You Really in the Moment?

Are we listening, are we rushing, and are we really concerned?

Therefore do not be anxious about tomorrow,
for tomorrow will be anxious for itself.
Sufficient for the day is its own trouble.

(Matthew 6:34, ESV)

Costumes Are
for Halloween

As I go through my day,
I begin to see that many
people are living life
with a costume on.

*Put on your new nature, and be
renewed as you learn to know your
Creator and become like him.*

(Colossians 3:10, NLT)

Leave It
and Move On

Going away provided
rest and renewal, and I
so appreciated that time,
but mostly, going away
reminded me of leaving it
all behind to gain Christ.

*No, dear brothers and sisters, I have
not achieved it, but I focus on this
one thing: Forgetting the past and
looking forward to what lies ahead.*

(Philippians 3:13, NLT)

His Love Will Bring You Back

Sometimes I drift, sometimes I am pulled into other dimensions, and sometimes I am torn, but He always draws me back to Him.

The LORD appeared to him from afar, saying, "I have loved you with an everlasting love; Therefore I have drawn you with lovingkindness."

(Jeremiah 31:3, NASB)

The Rhythm of Love

The closer I get to Him and the more I see from His perspective, the more the rhythm of my heart beats with His.

The glory that you have given me I have given to them, that they may be one even as we are one, I in them and you in me.

(John 17:22, ESV)

Turn Down
the Volume

Sometimes it takes
shutting off all the
voices that seek our
attention, and often
these voices have no
grasp or connection
to our journey.

*But when he, the Spirit of truth, comes, he
will guide you into all the truth. He will not
speak on his own; he will speak only what he
hears, and he will tell you what is yet to come.*

(John 16:13, NIV)

Your Words
Create Destiny

A harsh word can steal a dream; a good word can make one happen.

Let no corrupting talk come out of your mouths, but only such as is good for building up, as fits the occasion, that it may give grace to those who hear.

(Ephesians 4:29, ESV)

Imagine
There's No Heaven

Can you even for a
moment imagine life
without Him? No, I cannot
imagine life without Him.

I say to the LORD, "You are my Lord;
apart from you I have no good thing."

(Psalm 16:2, NIV)

Smile Brightly

When you smile
to a cashier in the
supermarket, or say thank
you to your postman, do
all you do knowing that
God's life in your actions
is ready to reach out to
a lonely soul who needs
the love you have inside.

Gracious words are like a honeycomb,
sweetness to the soul and health to the body.

(Proverbs 16:24, ESV)

Your Will or His?

Doing your own thing
sounds good, but if your
own thing is not His thing,
it will lead nowhere
and cost you dearly.

*For God is working in you, giving you the
desire and the power to do what pleases him.*

(Philippians 2:13, NLT)

A New Normal?

Things that were so
predictable have
become unpredictable,
and what was normal
seems so abnormal now. I
am grateful for the place
in Him, where light is light
and darkness is darkness.

*For God is not the author of
confusion, but of peace.*

(1 Corinthians 14:33, KJV)

My Eyes Are on You

Look to Him at all times. He will guide you, teach you, supply all your needs, contend with your enemies, make your paths straight, and make you more like Him. Yes, Lord, my eyes are on You.

For we are powerless against this great horde that is coming against us. We do not know what to do, but our eyes are on you.

(2 Chronicles 20:12, ESV)

Constant Wisdom

There are many things I'm not sure of, and all those things have variables. It's going to take a refusal of those variable things to live in what is constant.

Every good thing given and every perfect gift is from above, coming down from the Father of lights, with whom there is no variation or shifting shadow.

(James 1:17, NASB)

It Holds You Back

As I look at my life, every
day, I see things that I
need to put away, and
I know I'm not alone.
Help us, Holy Spirit, to
put away anything that
keeps us from being
marvelously transformed
into God's image.

*And to put on the new self, created to be like
God in true righteousness and holiness.*

(Ephesians 4:24, NIV)

Fixing My Gaze

There's always so much change in each day's journey. I do not understand, and neither do I ask why, for I know what matters most is to keep my eyes on the one who never changes; He is the stability of my times.

I keep my eyes always on the LORD. With him at my right hand, I will not be shaken.

(Psalm 16:8, NIV)

Team Player

The day I accepted Him into my life, I became a lifetime member of His body. It's sad that some who have accepted membership do not really want to participate like members but would rather be lone rangers.

We are many parts of one body, and we all belong to each other.

(Romans 12:5, NLT)

It's Not Worth It

I pray that we would
not chase after things
that rob us of life with no
eternal gain. Lord, give
us more grace to discern
lying vanities that try to
lure us into pathways
lighted not by You but
instead by artificial light.

*And what do you benefit if you gain the
whole world but lose your own soul? Is
anything worth more than your soul?*

(Matthew 16:26, NLT)

Christlike

We were created in His image and His likeness, so why should we settle for anything less? He is my constant, and my prayer is to consistently become more like Him.

And we all, who with unveiled faces contemplate the Lord's glory, are being transformed into his image with ever-increasing glory, which comes from the Lord, who is the Spirit.

(2 Corinthians 3:18, NIV)

Humility Leads to Greatness

Through humility Jesus was led to His ultimate victory, and as we humble ourselves to His purposes, in due time, we also will be lifted up and ushered into our destiny, to a place of hope and fruitfulness.

Humble yourselves therefore under the mighty hand of God, that he may exalt you in due time.

(1 Peter 5:6, KJV)

You're Better Than You Think

Thank You, Lord, for making each of us unique and important, with special gifts to enjoy and share with a world in need. We cannot do it alone.

From him the whole body, joined and held together by every supporting ligament, grows and builds itself up in love, as each part does its work.

(Ephesians 4:16, NIV)

Move Through Me

Beat in me, Lord, so that through me, You may beat in others.

He comforts us in all our troubles so that we can comfort others. When they are troubled, we will be able to give them the same comfort God has given us.

(2 Corinthians 1:4, NLT)

Spring Cleaning

I am needy, and each day my need for Him grows greater as I empty myself of anyone and anything in my life that attempts to settle for that which is not profitable, real, and purposeful.

If you try to hang on to your life, you will lose it. But if you give up your life for my sake, you will save it.

(Matthew 16:25, NLT)

The Choice
Is Yours

Sometimes the Lord may allow certain events to take place to get our attention so we become aware of a direction, but still the decisions are up to us.

If any of you lacks wisdom, you should ask God, who gives generously to all without finding fault, and it will be given to you.

(James 1:5, NIV)

Make My Desire
Your Desire

Life is way too short to
spend my days longing
for that which does
not long for me.

*Whom have I in heaven but You? And
besides You, I desire nothing on earth.*

(Psalm 73:25, NASB)

Replenish

It's a privilege to love others with the love of Christ, for when we give His love, God's love will flow through us and replenish our reservoir of hopes and dreams with His life.

Give, and it will be given to you. A good measure, pressed down, shaken together and running over, will be poured into your lap. For with the measure you use, it will be measured to you.

(Luke 6:38, NIV)

Unchanging

Oh, how I need Jesus. Oh, how I need His constant, unchanging, unwavering, predictable, steadfast love that never ceases to uphold me, that never ceases to amaze me.

For I am the LORD, I change not; therefore ye sons of Jacob are not consumed.

(Malachi 3:6, KJV)

So Faithful

He is our balance, our firm road, our constant lover who loves us even when we are not able to love Him.

If we are faithless, he remains faithful—
for he cannot deny himself.

(2 Timothy 2:13, ESV)

True Love?

When we say we love, we need to think twice about what we mean and what we say. Are we willing to truly love the way Christ loved us?

Greater love has no one than this, that one lay down his life for his friends. You are My friends if you do what I command you.

(John 15:13–14, NASB)

Staying Fixed on His Purpose

Let's pray: Lord, keep us on Your path, in Your ways, fixed to Your purpose. He will answer that prayer for you with much grace.

This is the confidence we have in approaching God: that if we ask anything according to his will, he hears us. And if we know that he hears us—whatever we ask—we know that we have what we asked of him.

(1 John 5:14-15, NIV)

Fear Is Not
from God

There are many things in
a day that seek to stop
my heartbeat that could
bring me to a place of
fear or hopelessness.
See the warning signs;
know that fear is not
God's mentality.

*For God hath not given us the
spirit of fear; but of power, and of
love, and of a sound mind.*

(2 Timothy 1:7, KJV)

Words Create Life

Speak His intentions. Speak words of encouragement, one to another. Always speak His outcomes, and they shall be unto you as you have spoken and believed.

Don't be drunk with wine, because that will ruin your life. Instead, be filled with the Holy Spirit, singing psalms and hymns and spiritual songs among yourselves, and making music to the Lord in your hearts.

(Ephesians 5:18–19, NLT)

Eternity Now

I am grateful that we may experience eternity now, in every breath with You.

Before the mountains were born Or You gave birth to the earth and the world, Even from everlasting to everlasting, You are God.

(Psalm 90:2, NASB)

Enter In

We all have an expiration date in this world. It's just not printed on us like it is on a milk carton. Let us therefore enter in to that place where there is no expiration date— the place where there is peace with God, the place of God's love.

The watchmen found me as they made their rounds in the city. "Have you seen the one my heart loves?" Scarcely had I passed them when I found the one my heart loves.

(Song of Songs 3:3-4, NIV)

Do What It Takes

I believe we are living in an hour where we need to ask ourselves the hard questions and then do whatever is necessary to stay on course with Him.

Watch and pray that you may not enter into temptation. The spirit indeed is willing, but the flesh is weak.

(Matthew 26:41, ESV)

Spirit or Flesh?

Sometimes life's journey
can take you to a place
of wondering who
and what to separate
yourself from and who
and what you need
to join yourself to.

*Those who live according to the flesh
have their minds set on what the
flesh desires; but those who live in
accordance with the Spirit have their
minds set on what the Spirit desires.*

(Romans 8:5, NIV)

Deeper Still

My heart's cry is for more
of Him, for I need to go
deeper, walk closer, and
listen. If you listen, you
will hear Him speak.

*Deep calls to deep in the roar of
your waterfalls; all your waves and
breakers have swept over me.*

(Psalm 42:7, NIV)

Obedience or Popularity?

Not everyone wants to swim upstream against the current, against popular opinion, and not all want to walk the straight and narrow way.

Do not love the world nor the things in the world. If anyone loves the world, the love of the Father is not in him.

(1 John 2:15, NASB)

Trust
Doesn't Just Happen

Trust takes time to
build. It's built line
upon line and precept
upon precept.

*Commit thy way unto the LORD; trust also
in him; and he shall bring it to pass.*

(Psalm 37:5, KJV)

Make the
Right Impression

Every day we get to
make choices that have
an impact on the heart
of another, and that
impact will make an
imprint that is lasting.

*So we are Christ's ambassadors; God is
making his appeal through us. We speak for
Christ when we plead, "Come back to God!"*

(2 Corinthians 5:20, NLT)

He Will
Take You There

There will always be
change, there will always
be opportunities, and
there will always be a
process we go through
to get to the other side.

They reeled and staggered like drunkards;
they were at their wits' end. Then they cried
out to the Lord in their trouble, and he brought
them out of their distress. He stilled the storm
to a whisper; the waves of the sea were
hushed. They were glad when it grew calm,
and he guided them to their desired haven.

(Psalm 107:27-30, NIV)

Words That Heal

Lord, allow the joy of salvation to flood our beings, to overtake our speech, and for healing to flow from our lips.

Gracious words are a honeycomb, sweet to the soul and healing to the bones.

(Proverbs 16:24, NIV)

Speak Life

Our words can carry
the hope of life or the
sting of death, so let
us always speak life
and hope to others.

*The soothing tongue is a tree of life, but
a perverse tongue crushes the spirit.*

(Proverbs 15:4, NIV)

Greatness Is in You

There are so many
people who need
what you have. Even
when you feel like you
have nothing, you
still have greatness
in you to impart. You
have Christ in you.

Because I live, you also will live. On that
day you will realize that I am in my Father,
and you are in me, and I am in you.

(John 14:19–20, NIV)

Joy Will Come

We can think something
is over and then there it is
again, or we can believe
we are over it when
suddenly it appears and
then tears begin again.

*Those who sow with tears will
reap with songs of joy.*

(Psalm 126:5, NIV)

Hope Again

I can remember when
I felt so stressed that I
felt like I was holding
my breath all the time,
and then suddenly there
would be someone who
would breathe on me,
and I would hope again.

*You who have made me see many troubles
and calamities will revive me again; from the
depths of the earth you will bring me up again.*

(Psalm 71:20, ESV)

Always Protected

Whatever the
unexpected event,
the Lord is forever a
constant shield about us,
leading us by still waters
and forever making
intercession for us.

*The LORD will guard your going out and your
coming in From this time forth and forever.*

(Psalm 121:8, NASB)

He Sees, He Hears

Sometimes life can just leave you speechless, and in those times, I am grateful that He interprets my tears.

You have kept count of my tossings; put my tears in your bottle. Are they not in your book?

(Psalm 56:8, ESV)

Held by God

He won't let us go, and
He won't allow us to
let Him go. Encourage
yourself in the Lord,
and know that you
are not forgotten.

*For I the LORD thy God will hold
thy right hand, saying unto thee,
Fear not; I will help thee.*

(Isaiah 41:13, KJV)

Forever

I'm amazed that
although there is a
beginning and an end
in this lifetime, our lives
with Him are forever.

*And this is the way to have eternal life—to
know you, the only true God, and Jesus
Christ, the one you sent to earth.*

(John 17:3, NLT)

Love Bait

We are His fishing rods, and the bait is His overwhelming, unfailing love.

Then Jesus said, "Come to me, all of you who are weary and carry heavy burdens, and I will give you rest. Take my yoke upon you. Let me teach you, because I am humble and gentle at heart, and you will find rest for your souls. For my yoke is easy to bear, and the burden I give you is light."

(Matthew 11:28–30, NLT)

There's Eternity in Your Giving

When you give, God is right there with you multiplying the force of your gift.

For God is the one who provides seed for the farmer and then bread to eat. In the same way, he will provide and increase your resources and then produce a great harvest of generosity in you.

(2 Corinthians 9:10, NLT)

The Lord Will Handle It

Some seasons are unexpected, uninvited, and unimaginable, yet they come in under the radar.

The LORD is good, A stronghold in the day of trouble, And He knows those who take refuge in Him.

(Nahum 1:7, NASB)

The Source and Director of Life

My greatest desire in life
is to know Him, hear Him,
and follow after Him,
for He is life to me and
without Him I am nothing.

*I cry out to God Most High, to God
who fulfills his purpose for me.*

(Psalm 57:2, ESV)

The Lord Wants
Your Burdens

Father, I thank You that
You can keep that which
we commit unto You,
and I pray that each
one of us will have grace
to commit the whole
of our cares to You,
knowing You care for us.

*Cast thy burden upon the LORD, and
he shall sustain thee: he shall never
suffer the righteous to be moved.*

(Psalm 55:22, KJV)

Don't Worry, He Knows

We trust in Your provision, for You know our every need, our every step, our every breath, our every aspiration.

I will answer them before they even call to me. While they are still talking about their needs, I will go ahead and answer their prayers!

(Isaiah 65:24, NLT)

The Red Light Means Stop

Some of us take the road less traveled while others find themselves on busy streets or stuck in traffic.

But the Lord answered her, "Martha, Martha, you are anxious and troubled about many things, but one thing is necessary. Mary has chosen the good portion, which will not be taken away from her."

(Luke 10:41–2, ESV)

Come Apart before You Come Apart

Challenges can shift our direction, interfere with our nights, and leave us sleepless, hopeless, and helpless.

Let all that I am wait quietly before God, for my hope is in him. He alone is my rock and my salvation, my fortress where I will not be shaken.

(Psalm 62:5–6, NLT)

He Can Part
Your Red Sea

Don't faint, don't give in
to the pressure, don't give
up, and whatever you
do, don't take situations
into your own hands.

*In fact, we expected to die. But as a result,
we stopped relying on ourselves and learned
to rely only on God, who raises the dead.*

(2 Corinthians 1:9–10, NLT)

Did God Really Say That?

There are things that happen in life's journey that cause us to get to a place of questioning Him.

Therefore I tell you, whatever you ask for in prayer, believe that you have received it, and it will be yours.

(Mark 11:24, NIV)

Destined
for a Good Life

God says yes to your
fulfillment, yes to your
joy, and yes to who
you are in Him.

*"For I know the plans I have for you,"
declares the LORD, "plans to prosper
you and not to harm you, plans to
give you hope and a future."*

(Jeremiah 29:11, NIV)

Confidence

Let us speak of His love,
His greatness, and
His ability to change
circumstances rather
than speak of the
despair we think we
face, but truly we don't.

*For I can do everything through
Christ, who gives me strength.*

(Philippians 4:13, NLT)

Sustained

When emotions run high,
they can cause me to
look down rather than
up, and in those times,
I remind myself that He
upholds all things, and
that includes me.

He is the radiance of the glory of God and the
exact imprint of his nature, and he upholds
the universe by the word of his power.

(Hebrews 1:3, ESV)

There's Always Hope

There is no feeling that He is not touched by and no infirmity He cannot heal.

Jesus went throughout Galilee, teaching in their synagogues, proclaiming the good news of the kingdom, and healing every disease and sickness among the people.

(Matthew 4:23, NIV)

There's a Time
to Let Go

I cared for and carried
many things and
people in my life's
journey that perhaps I
should have laid aside
earlier than I did, but I
thought I could help.

*Cast your bread upon the waters, for
you will find it after many days.*

(Ecclesiastes 11:1, ESV)

Serving
Is a Privilege

It makes me sad to see so
many looking for servants
when the greatest joy
in life comes from being
the one who serves.

It is more blessed to give than to receive.

(Acts 20:35, KJV)

Don't Give Up, God Is with You

Disappointments may come, but God will never disappoint us; He loves us and will move mountains in our way.

I will go before you and will level the mountains; I will break down gates of bronze and cut through bars of iron.

(Isaiah 45:2, NIV)

A Divine Reversal

Jesus brought about a new order, a new set of principles, and a new covenant that for some may be hard to follow but easy for those who accept Him.

Whoever exalts himself will be humbled, and whoever humbles himself will be exalted.

(Matthew 23:12, ESV)

Perspective

To be part of Him, like Him, and created in His infinite image gives me perspective for life.

I tell you the truth, anyone who believes in me will do the same works I have done, and even greater works, because I am going to be with the Father.

(John 14:12, NLT)

Kindness Turns Everything Around

Kindness heals. It brings hope. It will melt a bitter heart, dry our tears, and bring energy to a lifeless soul.

Because Your lovingkindness is better than life, My lips will praise You.

(Psalm 63:3, NASB)

Be
What You Desire

Be kind and you
shall reap what you
sow—a life of kindness,
a life of hope.

*Be kind and compassionate to one
another, forgiving each other, just
as in Christ God forgave you.*

(Ephesians 4:32, NIV)

Created

Before I was even
formed in the womb, He
conceived me, knew
me, hand-fashioned
me, and placed His
heartbeat and fingerprint
inside and upon me.

*For you created my inmost being; you
knit me together in my mother's womb.
Your eyes saw my unformed body; all the
days ordained for me were written in your
book before one of them came to be.*

(Psalm 139: 13–16, NIV)

Guided

I know the way I shall go because He directs me with His love.

I bless the LORD who gives me counsel; in the night also my heart instructs me. I have set the LORD always before me; because he is at my right hand, I shall not be shaken.

(Psalm 16:7–8, ESV)

Unlimited

His potential in us is boundless, offering possibilities of grace and hope everywhere we shine His light.

Now to him who is able to do immeasurably more than all we ask or imagine, according to his power that is at work within us, to him be glory in the church and in Christ Jesus throughout all generations, for ever and ever! Amen.

(Ephesians 3:20–21, NIV)

Praise Him

It's easy to be joyful or hopeful when things are going great, but miracles happen when we wait on the Lord and praise Him.

I will praise you, Lord my God, with all my heart; I will glorify your name forever.

(Psalm 86:12, NIV)

Eyes of Faith

When we don't see visible proof, we can take advantage of the glorious opportunity to praise Him for what He's doing that we do not see.

Though you have not seen him, you love him; and even though you do not see him now, you believe in him and are filled with an inexpressible and glorious joy.

(1 Peter 1:8, NIV)

It Will Happen

Often, disappointments will cause us to miss the time of our visitation by focusing on disappointment rather than His appointed time of destiny.

For the vision is yet for the appointed time; It hastens toward the goal and it will not fail. Though it tarries, wait for it; For it will certainly come, it will not delay.

(Habakkuk 2:3, NASB)

We Need Certainty

Regardless of the circumstance, it's always the certainty found in Him that will guard our hearts and minds against all fear.

For I am convinced that neither death nor life, neither angels nor demons, neither the present nor the future, nor any powers, neither height nor depth, nor anything else in all creation, will be able to separate us from the love of God that is in Christ Jesus our Lord.

(Romans 8:38–39, NIV)

Abundant Supply

His goodness, His mercy,
His faithfulness, His love,
and the magnitude of
His grace are always
more than sufficient.

*They feast on the abundance of
your house, and you give them drink
from the river of your delights.*

(Psalm 36:8, ESV)

There's More

Life is beautiful and full of wonder, so I wonder why at times we lose sight of Him working behind the scenes.

By faith we understand that the universe was created by the word of God, so that what is seen was not made out of things that are visible.

(Hebrews 11:3, ESV)

You're Covered

I must be able to find Him in the midst of chaos and know that He is faithful.

You are my hiding place; You preserve me from trouble; You surround me with songs of deliverance.

(Psalm 32:7, NASB)

To Give
or Not to Give

Stop to listen, hear
His voice, and don't
doubt that which
you know to do or
withhold good while it
is within you to do it.

*One person gives freely, yet gains
even more; another withholds
unduly, but comes to poverty.*

(Proverbs 11:24, NIV)

Clear Lines Go
to the Finish Line

I need strong boundaries, clear lines, and constants I can count on.

The precepts of the LORD are right, rejoicing the heart; The commandment of the LORD is pure, enlightening the eyes.

(Psalm 19:8, ESV)

Supernatural Direction

We see through a glass darkly and we only know in part, so we are bound to get lost without the other part—God's part.

This foolish plan of God is wiser than the wisest of human plans, and God's weakness is stronger than the greatest of human strength.

(1 Corinthians 1:25, NLT)

So You Think You Know Better?

I wonder how we get to the place of I'll do it my way or I know what's best.

I am the LORD your God, who teaches you to profit, who leads you in the way you should go.

(Isaiah 48:17, ESV)

Be the Answer

I don't know what's set
before you, but I do know
we all have something
before us, and I pray
that, regardless, He
will answer your prayer
while making you the
answer for another.

*For the creation waits in eager expectation
for the children of God to be revealed.*

(Romans 8:19, NIV)

Frustrated?

When Christ said to the apostle Paul, "It is hard for thee to kick against the pricks" (Acts 26:14 KJV), Christ was saying, Why are you fighting against My will?

He has shown you, O mortal, what is good. And what does the LORD require of you? To act justly and to love mercy and to walk humbly with your God.

(Micah 6:8, NIV)

The Choice Is Clear

The decision we get to
make in the change is
whether we will change
for the better or not
and whether we will do
it our way or His way.

*Patient endurance is what you need now, so
that you will continue to do God's will. Then
you will receive all that he has promised.*

(Hebrews 10:36, NLT)

Keep It Simple

When it gets complicated, you can count me out.

I am leaving you with a gift—peace of mind and heart. And the peace I give is a gift the world cannot give. So don't be troubled or afraid.

(John 14:27, NLT)

Don't Let It Pass You By

Too many times we let
precious thoughts, deeds
to be done, or seeds
to be planted pass us
by, and we miss the
timing of our visitation
to be a blessing and
to get the job done.

*For we are God's handiwork, created in
Christ Jesus to do good works, which
God prepared in advance for us to do.*

(Ephesians 2:10, NIV)

The Fruit
of Your Lips

I stand with you today
to never speak "never"
over your life again,
because many times in
doing so, your "never"
robs you of your future.

*Death and life are in the power of the tongue,
and those who love it will eat its fruits.*

(Proverbs 18:21, ESV)

Cling to Hope

Life's journey is a learning experience, and we must learn to keep living, keep believing, keep trusting, and never stop hoping.

But you, take courage! Do not let your hands be weak, for your work shall be rewarded.

(2 Chronicles 15:7, ESV)

Know Him

Be aware of Him, listen
for His voice, see His
light in your waking, feel
His comfort all around
you, and know His
heartbeat in your soul.

*You make known to me the path of life; in
your presence there is fullness of joy; at
your right hand are pleasures forevermore.*

(Psalm 16:11, ESV)

Life-Changing Words

Speak virtuous, life-giving power from His Word, receive the miracle energy of God, and then break through into a life of destiny, a life of hope, of hope fulfilled.

So is my word that goes out from my mouth: it will not return to me empty, but will accomplish what I desire and achieve the purpose for which I sent it.

(Isaiah 55:11, NIV)

Have Faith;
God Will Bring It

When we remain open
to the new occurrences
of each day, we will
find them because
He will make sure
that they find us.

*And without faith it is impossible to please
God, because anyone who comes to him
must believe that he exists and that he
rewards those who earnestly seek him.*

(Hebrews 11:6, NIV)

Everywhere

There is a divine exchange in every breath, a wonder in every experience, a purpose in every event, and the life of God in all we do.

One God and Father of all, who is above all, and through all, and in you all.

(Ephesians 4:6, KJV)

A Chain Reaction

When you do praise
Him for what He gives,
others will see Him and
give thanks for all the
goodness He creates.

*You will be enriched in every way to be
generous in every way, which through
us will produce thanksgiving to God.*

(2 Corinthians 9:11, ESV)

Great Expectation

I find it vital not to look at my days as the same old, same old thing but instead with great expectation.

There is surely a future hope for you, and your hope will not be cut off.

(Proverbs 23:18, NIV)

God Is a Giver

There is nothing impossible with God in each day, and there is nothing He will withhold from those He loves.

For the LORD God is a sun and shield: the LORD will give grace and glory: no good thing will he withhold from them that walk uprightly.

(Psalm 84:11, KJV)

In Him

May intimacy with You be our hearts' cry, for it is in that place that we experience the depth of Your love, and it is in that place where we are sound and safe and know all is well.

Abide in me, and I in you. As the branch cannot bear fruit by itself, unless it abides in the vine, neither can you, unless you abide in me.

(John 15:4, ESV)

The Lord Answers

Many of us are crying
out. In fact, I believe
all of us have a special
heart cry we are longing
for. Although His answer
may tarry, it is vital
that we continue to
call out to Him, for He
is faithful to answer.

*In my desperation I prayed, and the Lord
listened; he saved me from all my troubles.*

(Psalm 34:6, NLT)

Find True Rest

I love the sun, but I love the Son more. There is never a cloud too thick to cover the glory of His Son. He gives as we enter into His rest—a true rest, in Him—that heals, loves, and soothes our deepest wounds.

Yes, my soul, find rest in God; my hope comes from him. Truly he is my rock and my salvation; he is my fortress, I will not be shaken.

(Psalm 62:6, NIV)

Lean on Me

As the hymn writer exclaimed, "Leaning, leaning, safe and secure from all alarms; Leaning, leaning, leaning on the everlasting arms."

The eternal God is your refuge, and underneath are the everlasting arms.

(Deuteronomy 33:27, NIV)

The Lord
Will Show You

Thank You, Lord, for hearing, for answering, for showing us things we know not. May Your voice be the loudest in our ears, and may our answer always be, Yes, Lord, I surrender all.

Call unto me, and I will answer thee,
and shew thee great and mighty
things, which thou knowest not.

(Jeremiah 33:3, KJV)

Are You Running to Him?

The question, "A wounded spirit who can bear?" I believe is answered by the spirit of the person who knows Him, runs to Him, and who always casts his or her cares on Him.

In the morning, O LORD, You will hear my voice; In the morning I will order my prayer to You and eagerly watch.

(Psalm 5:3, NASB)

Not Forgotten

He knows when you seek Him and makes Himself found, and He opens the door when you knock.

Then he continued, "Do not be afraid, Daniel. Since the first day that you set your mind to gain understanding and to humble yourself before your God, your words were heard, and I have come in response to them."

(Daniel 10:12, NIV)

Ask and Receive

He will not leave you hungry, He will not leave you thirsty, and He will not ignore your heartfelt pleas. He hears and answers when we ask.

So I say to you: Ask and it will be given to you; seek and you will find; knock and the door will be opened to you.

(Luke 11: 9, NIV)

Constant
Revelations

He is constantly speaking
and always leading us
into truth. I will never
stop listening and
never stop following.

The heavens declare the glory of God;
the skies proclaim the work of his hands.
Day after day they pour forth speech;
night after night they reveal knowledge.

(Psalm 19:1–2, NIV)

Straight from the Throne

There is such a huge difference between a message and a word from God. I compare them to fast food against a home-cooked meal.

And we also thank God constantly for this, that when you received the word of God, which you heard from us, you accepted it not as the word of men but as what it really is, the word of God, which is at work in you believers.

(1 Thessalonians 2:13, ESV)

Speak Life

Our words will heal and will make the unloved feel loved.

The words of the reckless pierce like swords,
but the tongue of the wise bring healing.

(Proverbs 12:18, NIV)

Share It

Giving what we have strengthens the weak, gives hope to the hopeless, and gives purpose to those who have no vision.

Heal the sick, raise the dead, cure those with leprosy, and cast out demons. Give as freely as you have received!

(Matthew 10:8, NLT)

In His Arms

In my weakness He is strong, and knowing He is with me makes all the difference.

He will feed his flock like a shepherd. He will carry the lambs in his arms, holding them close to his heart. He will gently lead the mother sheep with their young.

(Isaiah 40:11, NLT)

Move Mountains

Faith-filled words can move mountains, call things that are not as though they are, still storms, comfort the soul, heal, and especially proclaim the eternal good news.

Truly, I say to you, whoever says to this mountain, 'Be taken up and thrown into the sea,' and does not doubt in his heart, but believes that what he says will come to pass, it will be done for him.

(Mark 11:23, ESV)

Stay in It

When I was a kid, I would invest my time walking around with a shopping cart collecting bottles to return for money. It was worth it to me, so I put the time in.

Let us not become weary in doing good, for at the proper time we will reap a harvest if we do not give up.

(Galatians 6:9, NIV)

Plant for a Harvest

I believe life is about making investments, and without an investment, there has to be an understanding that there will be no return.

I said, "Plant the good seeds of righteousness, and you will harvest a crop of love. Plow up the hard ground of your hearts, for now is the time to seek the Lord, that he may come and shower righteousness upon you."

(Hosea 10:12, NLT)

A Win-Win
Situation

In all of my losses, He
has been my gain, and
in all of my gain, He
has still been my gain.

*More than that, I count all things to be loss
in view of the surpassing value of knowing
Christ Jesus my Lord, for whom I have
suffered the loss of all things, and count
them but rubbish so that I may gain Christ,*

(Philippians 3:8, NASB)

We Become
Like Him

Some days it seems
as though the process
will kill me, and then I
realize it's the process
that's making me,
shaping me, changing
me, and molding me
as I seek to embrace
His will in all things.

*He must become greater and greater,
and I must become less and less.*

(John 3:30, NLT)

It's Never Too Late

It's never too late for anyone to turn around and to turn back to their love. Though they may walk east for fifty years, to go west, all they have to do is turn around.

Return to the LORD your God, for he is merciful and compassionate, slow to get angry and filled with unfailing love. He is eager to relent and not punish.

(Joel 2:13, NLT)

The Real Treasure

Lord, give us grace to make You our treasure and not the world. May we all come to a place of contentment in You that adds increase to the time we are here, for truly our days are numbered.

But godliness with contentment is great gain. For we brought nothing into the world, and we can take nothing out of it.

(1 Timothy 6:6–7, NIV)

Free to Be

I am so thankful for a
life of freedom. I am
free—free to see as He
sees, free to do as He
does, free to be the me
He created me to be.
I am thankful, Lord, for
this life of grace You
have so freely given.

*Now the Lord is the Spirit, and where the
Spirit of the Lord is, there is freedom.*

(2 Corinthians 3:17, NIV)

Discern the Times

I pray we would consider
our ways in the light of
His Word and not in the
opinions of others. We
must discern the times,
discern our activities,
and take on His yoke,
which fits us perfectly.

*Take my yoke upon you and learn from
me, for I am gentle and humble in heart,
and you will find rest for your souls.*

(Matthew 11:29, NIV)

A New Light

I see Him in everything.
It's the only way I know
how to live! I must get
His perspective in all
things. If I don't, there's
no hope, no reason, no
purpose, but with Him
all things become new.

Open my eyes, that I may behold
Wonderful things from Your law.

(Psalm 119:18, NASB)

Guard Your Heart

Help us, Lord, to hold back the tide of troubles from seeping into the hidden places of our hearts, for this onslaught seeks to steal our prized possessions: our faith, hope, and love.

Above all else, guard your heart, for everything you do flows from it.

(Proverbs 4:23, NIV)

Share the Love

Hug someone today, and make sure it's a hug from the inside out that changes someone from the outside in and changes both of you by the power of His Spirit.

He comforts us in all our troubles so that we can comfort others. When they are troubled, we will be able to give them the same comfort God has given us.

(2 Corinthians 1:3–4, NLT)

Constant Stability

There is much I thought was stable, secure, and solid, yet there were times of great instability where natural security was not to be found. Yet when all is said and done, He alone remains the same, stable, and secure.

For in him we live, and move, and have our being;

(Acts 17:28, KJV)

Follow Peace

When I follow after God's
word and His peace,
I'm never at a loss, even
when there's a fork in
the road. His way is
always clear, and His
Word is always sure.

*And the peace of God, which surpasses
all understanding, will guard your hearts
and your minds in Christ Jesus.*

(Philippians 4:7, ESV)

Listen and Receive

As we travel upon
this earthly voyage,
our opportunities are
boundless. Every day is
a gift, every heartbeat is
a miracle, and in every
choice, in every beat,
it's vital to hear His voice
and know His way.

Lead me in Your truth and teach me,
For You are the God of my salvation;
For You I wait all the day.

(Psalm 25:5, NASB)

The Only Way

May we all find grace
to answer, "Yes, Lord,"
to Your will, to Your way,
and to Your leading as
we follow You all our
days in the surrender
of Your love. Lord, You
lead and we will follow.

Teach me to do your will, for you are my God!
Let your good Spirit lead me on level ground!

(Psalm 143:10, ESV)

Stay Close

When I made a decision
to follow Him, there were
choices to be made,
and now I recognize
never to go before Him,
never to go out in front
of Him, and never to get
too far behind Him.

*And your ears shall hear a word behind you,
saying, "This is the way, walk in it," when you
turn to the right or when you turn to the left.*

(Isaiah 30:21, ESV)

Unseen Perspective

When I have the right
perspective on things, not
letting go of His peace,
I am able to keep my
cool, and life continues
to flow uninterrupted by
the annoyances and
noise in the journey.

*So we fix our eyes not on what is seen, but
on what is unseen, since what is seen is
temporary, but what is unseen is eternal.*

(2 Corinthians 4:18, NIV)

Divinely Centered

Some seasons take
me to a place where
I feel misunderstood
and unglued. In
these seasons, I am
kept together by a
divine desire to share
kindness with others
who feel misunderstood
in their journey.

*May the Lord now show you kindness and
faithfulness, and I too will show you the
same favor because you have done this.*

(2 Samuel 2:6, NIV)

Stuff Happens

Stuff happens, and when it does, you just have to push through. Don't let it grip you or get to your heart. When we are living in Him, things will come and things will go, but He remains.

Jesus Christ is the same yesterday, today and forever

(Hebrews 13:8, NLT)

It Will Be Okay

In all the small and big moments, I trust my God. If I miss a train, miss a plane, or lose an opportunity, His Word has taught me to trust that He has everything under control.

I make known the end from the beginning, from ancient times, what is still to come. I say, "My purpose will stand, and I will do all that I please."

(Isaiah 46:10, NIV)

Seeing
Is Not Believing

We must learn to trust
Him when we feel
like we cannot trace
Him. Often I can hear
myself say, "Lord, where
are You in this? Why
is this happening?"

*Jesus said to him, "Have you
believed because you have seen
me? Blessed are those who have
not seen and yet have believed."*

(John 20:29, ESV)

He's
All about Us

He never sleeps, He never slumbers, and even though it's all about Him, He's all about us!

What is the price of five sparrows—two copper coins? Yet God does not forget a single one of them. And the very hairs on your head are all numbered. So don't be afraid; you are more valuable to God than a whole flock of sparrows.

(Luke 12:6–7, NLT)

About the Cover Designer
Kristine Cotterman

The front and back cover graphic design was created by Kris Cotterman of Exodus Design Studios. **www.exodusdesign.com**

Since March of 1998, Exodus Design has grown to serve hundreds of clients throughout the U.S. and the world. Kris says: "Our success was built on faith."

About the Photographer
Albaner C. Eugene Jr.

Albaner C. Eugene Jr. captured the Author's Cover Photo at the Love of Jesus Family Church. Albaner says: "Victory is a result of a relationship with God. If we have a relationship with a victorious God, then victory becomes a life style." Albaner's ministry expressions can be viewed on YouTube.

About the Artist
Noelle S. Gibbons

The cover illustration was painted by Noelle S. Gibbons.

Noelle S. Gibbons has been drawing ever since she could pick up a pencil. At an early age, Noelle knew she wanted to use her God-given gift for His glory. Noelle is a commission artist, a private teacher, and has illustrated *The Lowdown on the High Bridge*, a children's book. She is blessed to live in Iowa with her husband and young son.

Noelle's website: Artbynoelle.com

About the Graphic Artists
Jason and Zhay Smith

Jason and Zhay Smith have provided graphic consultation and design expertise in the ongoing process of making Gale's books and marketing materials.

Jason and Zhay Smith are a husband-and-wife graphic team working to provide creative visual solutions to businesses in the New York metro area. They have over fifteen years of experience designing logos, package design, and stationary and event design collateral. They reside in Westchester County, New York, with their son.

About the Creative Associate
Julio Vitolo

Julio Vitolo grew up in the Bronx, New York, not too far from the Yankee Stadium. He graduated from the City College of New York with a degree in early childhood education and music. As a corridor teacher in an innovative Manhattan school setting, he acquired a keen instinct to recognize and develop the unique gifting within each child.

Subsequently, he applied his creative, educational instincts to business and successfully helped people develop their special interests.

Julio gives credit to his early educational roots: *Inspiring & nurturing children has taught me how to identify, brand, and develop something tangible from a seed of an idea to completion.*

As an inspired saxophonist, Julio shares his spiritual inclinations through his gift of music. In all his endeavours, he is passionate about touching others with the love of God and is instinctively driven to help others reach their full, God-given dreams and potential.

Julio's Facebook page is: Julio Vee.

About the Author
Gale Alvarez

Thirty years of dedicated, hands-to-the-plough ministry as cofounder and copastor of the Love of Jesus Family Church combined with ten thousand hidden acts of kindness that multitudes and heaven know of are the treasures that make up the precious woman of God, Gale Alvarez.

Inside and outside her church, Gale delivers the Word of God with compassion, prophetic precision, and timely accuracy. Outside of the sanctuary walls, she lives her life in selfless abandonment, giving her time and sharing her resources, her pure faith, and her love to the masses of humanity with whom she comes into contact. Her devotion is endless, and her heart is wide open to receive from God as she gives back to others.

Thank you, Gale, for displaying the beauty that only He can make from the ashes of our lives. Thank you for being an example of a living sacrifice. I am honored to know her and to be loved by her and to share in life's journey together.

Dr. Dawn Chillon, PhD, LPC
founder, The Foundation for Family Healing

Gale Alvarez pours out of her very being and her life experience to engage people where they live.

Valerie J. Fullilove, Writer/Producer
Trinity Park Productions

Pastor Gale is a visionary with integrity and sterling character. From her gentle elegance, but firm, confident voice, flow volumes of wisdom.

Bettye Blackston
director, The Women of Purpose Ministry

The healing ointment that comes from Gale's special journey is a sweet savor to God.

Dr. Gerald G. Loyd
Fountain of Life International Fellowship

If you sit more than two minutes with Gale, you will hear the heartbeat of God.

Reverend Pat Higgins
Restoration Family Church, Hillside, New Jersey

Gale Alvarez is a woman who puts her actions where her intentions are—just amazing.

Pastor Cassiaus Farrell
founder, The Love of Jesus Family Church,
Patterson, New Jersey

There has never been a time when Pastor Gale hasn't spoken directly to my heart. We are thankful for her compassion, commitment, and dedication to the people of God.

Pastor Barbara Glanton
The Love of Jesus Family Church, Newark,
New Jersey

It is evident that Gale has taken the circumstances that life has served her as opportunities to find God and ever press into a greater love and knowledge of the Most High!

Barry E. Taylor
founder, Liberty Ministries Inc.

Gale welcomes your responses and would love to hear your impressions.

Gale's Facebook page is:
Gale Alvarez HeartBeats

Gale is also available for speaking and ministry engagements at:
973-676-4200

Gale's e-mail: galewop@aol.com

Thank you!

The Ministry of Gale Alvarez

Personal Impressions

_____

_____

_____

_____

_____

_____

_____

_____

_____

_____

_____

_____

_____

_____

Personal Impressions

_____

_____

_____

_____

_____

_____

_____

_____

_____

_____

_____

_____

_____

_____

_____

_____

_____

Personal Impressions

Personal Impressions

Personal Impressions

———————————————————

———————————————————

———————————————————

———————————————————

———————————————————

———————————————————

———————————————————

———————————————————

———————————————————

———————————————————

———————————————————

———————————————————

———————————————————

———————————————————

———————————————————

———————————————————

Personal Impressions

Personal Impressions

_____

_____

_____

_____

_____

_____

_____

_____

_____

_____

_____

_____

_____

_____

_____

Personal Impressions

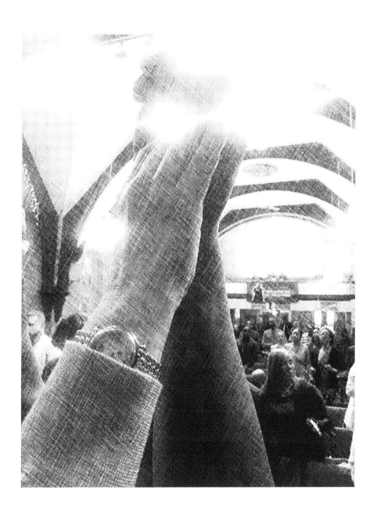

Printed in the United States
By Bookmasters